Design: Judith Chant and Alison Lee
Recipe Photography: Peter Barry
Jacket and Illustration Artwork: Jane Winton, courtesy of
Bernard Thornton Artists, London
Editor: Josephine Bacon

CHARTWELL BOOKS
a division of Book Sales, Inc.
POST OFFICE BOX 7100
114 Northfield Avenue
Edison, NJ 08818-7100

CLB 4260

© 1995 CLB Publishing, Godalming, Surrey, U.K.

Printed and bound in Singapore

ISBN 0-7858-0236-3

THE LITTLE BOOK
· OF ·

Mexican Cooking

The perfect introduction to the delights of Mexican cooking.

CHARTWELL
BOOKS, INC.

Introduction

Mexican food flavors are flamboyant and exciting yet the cooking techniques are simple and the ingredients inexpensive and readily available. There are plenty of fresh vegetables and cheeses, and the meats are generally slow-cooked, making them easily digestible. Mexican food is much more varied than the standard restaurant offerings would have you believe. Each state of Mexico has its own style of cuisine, as do those states of the United States that were once Mexican – California, Texas, Arizona and New Mexico. Tex-Mex is often dismissed as being uninteresting, yet it can be a style as authentically Mexican as anything produced south of the Rio Grande.

The recipes in this book include those simple basic dishes which we all associate with Mexican cooking – Burritos, Chili con Carne, Chimichangas, and Enchiladas. In addition, there are some exciting regional dishes such as Shrimp Veracruz and Moyettes, and delicious desserts such as Mango Whip and Chocolate Flan which are not quite so well-known. The essential side-dishes – Guacamole, Taco Sauce, and Flour Tortillas feature here too. Once you have acquired the knack of making flour tortillas, rolling them out deftly and quickly with a small rolling pin made from a piece of broom handle, like the Mexicans do, you can soon graduate to making your own corn tortillas. It takes some practice to make the *masa harina* just wet enough to hold together, and to roll them out just right (or you can use a tortilla press) but the result is worth the effort. Tortillas should always be eaten hot and fresh as possible, and they should always be kept wrapped in cloth until eaten.

A word about the cheeses mentioned in these recipes. Although yellow or Jack cheese is suggested as the cheese to use, you can also use sharp cheddar, or if your taste buds can stand it, jalapeno cheese. There are also some delicious Mexican cheeses you can try, such as queso menonito and queso ranchero.

Of course, all Mexican savory dishes require chilies. Specific types of chili are not mentioned, as the availability varies from place to place. Generally, fresh chilies are sharper than dried ones. The hottest chile is *chile pequin. Chile California* (Anaheim chili) and *chile Serrano* are milder, and the black and brown chilies such as *chile ancho*, are milder still. Mexican chili powder contains chili mixed with other spices, always including coriander (cilantro). Experiment with the amount of chili powder and fresh chilies until you have a mixture that is not too hot for you, your family and guests. Always wash your hands before and after handling raw chilies, wear plastic or rubber gloves when cutting them, and do not put your hands near your eyes – chilies are a powerful irritant.

You will find that home-cooked Mexican food is at least as delicious as anything you can eat in a restaurant, and is generally healthier and more nutritious. Use these recipes as a guide to the basics of Mexican cuisine and a springboard for creating your own exciting Mexican dishes.

Guacamole

SERVES 8

This is one of Mexico's most famous dishes. It is delicious as a first course on its own or as an ingredient in other recipes.

PREPARATION: 25 mins

1 medium onion, finely chopped
1 clove garlic, crushed
Grated rind and juice of ½ lime
½ quantity Taco Sauce (see recipe)
3 large ripe avocados
Salt and black pepper
1 tbsp chopped fresh coriander (cilantro)
Coriander (cilantro) leaves, to garnish
Tortilla chips, to serve

1. Mix the onion, garlic, rind and juice of the lime, and the taco sauce together in a large bowl.

2. Cut the avocados in half lengthwise. Twist the halves gently in opposite directions to separate.

Step 2 Cut the avocados in half lengthwise and twist the halves in opposite directions to separate.

Step 3 Hit the stone with a large knife and twist to remove.

3. Hit the stone with the blade of a large, sharp knife, and twist the knife to remove the stone.

4. Place the avocado halves cut side down on a chopping board. Lightly score the skin lengthwise and gently pull back to peel. Alternatively, scoop out avocado flesh with a spoon, scraping the skin well.

5. Chop the avocado coarsely and immediately place in the bowl with the onion and lime.

6. Use a potato masher to break up the avocado until almost smooth. Do not over-mash. Season, and stir in the chopped coriander (cilantro). Spoon into a serving bowl and garnish with coriander (cilantro) leaves.

7. Surround the bowl with tortilla chips for dipping.

Burritos

SERVES 6

Burritos are filled with a bean mixture, to which cooked, shredded beef or pork can be added.

PREPARATION: 25 mins
COOKING: 20 mins

6 Flour Tortillas (see recipe)
1 onion, chopped
1 tbsp oil
1 pound canned refried beans
6 lettuce leaves, shredded
½ cup Yellow or Jack cheese, grated
2 tomatoes, sliced
2 tbsps snipped chives
Full quantity Taco Sauce recipe
1¼ cups sour cream
Chopped coriander (cilantro) leaves

1. Wrap the tortillas in aluminum foil and heat in a warm oven to soften them.

2. Cook the onion in the oil until soft but not colored. Add the beans and heat through.

3. Spoon the mixture down the center of each

Step 3 Fold in the ends and sides of each tortilla over the filling to make rectangular packages.

warm tortilla. Top with the lettuce, cheese, tomatoes, and chives. Fold over the sides to form long rectangular packages. Make sure the filling is completely enclosed.

4. Place the burritos in an ovenproof dish, cover and cook in an oven preheated to 350°F, about 20 minutes.

5. Spoon the hot taco sauce over the burritos. Top with the sour cream and sprinkle with chopped coriander (cilantro) to serve.

Moyettes

SERVES 4

*These sandwiches are very popular for
breakfast in Mexico. Other types of yellow cheese can be used in the filling.*

PREPARATION: 15 mins
COOKING: 20 mins

4 crusty bread rolls
2 tbsps butter or margarine
1 cup canned refried beans
2 green onions (scallions), chopped
4 tbsps grated Jack or American cheese

1. Cut the rolls in half and remove some of the insides.

Step 1 Remove some of the insides of each roll, using a teaspoon or small knife.

Step 3 Fill the bottom halves of the rolls with the refried beans.

2. Soften the butter and spread on the insides of the rolls.

3. Fill the bottom halves of the rolls with the refried beans.

4. Sprinkle with the green onion (scallion) and top with the grated cheese then the bread "lids."

5. Place the rolls on a cookie sheet and cook in an oven preheated to 325°F for 15-20 minutes until the cheese has melted and the beans are hot. Serve immediately.

Chimichangas

SERVES 6

A strange sounding name for a delicious snack which is something like a deep-fried taco.

PREPARATION: 30 mins
COOKING: 18 mins

6 Flour Tortillas (see recipe)
Half quantity Chili Con Carne recipe
6 lettuce leaves, shredded
6 green onions (scallions), chopped
½ cup Yellow or Jack cheese, grated
Oil, for frying
Half quantity Guacamole recipe
1¼ cups sour cream
1 tomato, seeded and chopped

1. Wrap the tortillas in aluminum foil and place in a warm oven for 5 minutes to make them pliable.

2. Heat the chili briefly and spoon about 2

Step 3 Fold the tortillas over the filling to enclose completely and form packages.

Step 4 Lower the packages into the hot oil folded side first.

tbsps onto the center of each tortilla. Top with the lettuce, green onions (scallions), and cheese.

3. Fold in the sides to make packages making sure all the filling is enclosed.

4. Heat about 1-inch of oil in a large skillet and when hot, lower in the chimichangas, folded side downward. Cook 2-4 at a time, depending on the size of the skillet.

5. Cook 3 minutes and carefully turn over. Cook a further 3 minutes, remove to kitchen paper, and drain. Repeat with the remaining chimichangas.

6. Spoon the guacamole over the top of each and drizzle with the sour cream. Sprinkle with the chopped tomato and serve immediately.

Nachos

SERVES 8-10

Nachos make excellent cocktail savories; the variety of toppings and flavor combinations is almost endless.

PREPARATION: 20 mins
COOKING: 25 mins

Beef filling
2 tsps oil
8 ounces ground beef
½ onion, chopped
1-2 tsps chili powder
Pinch of ground coriander (cilantro)
Pinch of cayenne pepper
Salt and pepper

1 pack round tortilla chips
1 can refried beans
Full quantity Taco Sauce recipe
1 can Jalapeño bean dip
8-10 cherry tomatoes, sliced
½ cup sour cream or plain yogurt
Black and stuffed green olives, sliced
Yellow or Jack cheese, grated

---

1. Heat the oil for the beef filling in a skillet and brown the ground beef and onion,

breaking the meat up as it cooks. Add the spices and seasoning and cook about 20 minutes.

2. Top half of the tortilla chips with the refried beans and half with the beef filling.

3. Place 1 tbsp of taco sauce on the bean-topped chips and Jalapeño bean dip in the beef-topped chips.

4. Top the nachos with tomatoes, sour cream or yogurt, olives, or cheese in any combination, and serve.

Step 4 Top the nachos with tomatoes, sour cream, olives or cheese, as preferred and serve.

Taco Sauce

MAKES 1¼ cups

This basic recipe has many uses in Mexican cooking – sauce, topping, dip, or as an ingredient to give a dish extra flavor.

PREPARATION: 20 mins
COOKING: 10 mins

---

1 tbsp oil
1 onion, diced
1 green bell pepper, diced
½–1 red or green chili
½ tsp ground cumin
½ tsp ground coriander (cilantro)
1 clove garlic, crushed
Pinch of salt, pepper and sugar
14-ounce can tomatoes
Tomato paste (optional)

---

1. Heat the oil in a heavy-based saucepan and when hot, add the onion and pepper. Cook slowly to soften slightly.

2. Chop the chili and add with the cumin, coriander (cilantro) and garlic and cook a further 2-3 minutes.

3. Add sugar, seasonings, and the tomatoes with their juice.

4. Cook for a further 5-6 minutes over a

Step 2 Cut the chili in half, removing the seeds if wished, and chop the flesh finely.

Step 3 Add the sugar, seasonings, and the tomatoes to the pan and use a fork or wooden spoon to break up the tomatoes.

moderate heat to reduce and thicken slightly. Add the tomato paste for color, if necessary. Adjust the seasoning, and use hot or cold according to your recipe.

Flour Tortillas

MAKES 12

Flour tortillas are easier to make at home than the corn variety. Always use a very light rolling-pin, a short length of broom handle is ideal.

PREPARATION: 60 mins
COOKING: 5 mins

---

4 cups all-purpose flour
1 tbsp salt
⅓ cup lard or shortening
About 1¼ cups hot water

---

1. Sift the flour and salt into a mixing bowl and rub in the lard or shortening until the mixture resembles fine breadcrumbs. Gradually mix in enough of the water to form a soft, pliable dough.

2. Knead on a well-floured surface until smooth and no longer sticky. Cover with a damp kitchen towel.

Step 2 Knead the dough on a floured surface until smooth and pliable.

Step 4 Roll each ball of dough out very thinly and cut out a 10-inch circle.

3. Cut off about 3 tbsps of dough at a time, keeping the rest covered. Knead into a ball.

4. Roll the ball of dough out into a very thin circle, using a floured rolling pin. Cut into a neat round, using a 10-inch plate as a guide. Continue until all the dough has been used.

5. Stack the tortillas as you make them, flouring each well to prevent sticking. Cover with a clean tea-towel.

6. Heat a large heavy-based skillet and carefully place one tortilla in it. Cook about 10 seconds per side. Stack the tortillas and keep them covered until all are cooked.

Tacos

MAKES 12

Ready-made taco shells make this famous Mexican snack easy to prepare.

PREPARATION: 40 mins
COOKING: 20 mins

---

12 taco shells

Beef filling
Double quantity beef filling recipe for Nachos

Chicken filling
3 tbsps butter or margarine
1 onion, chopped
1 small red bell pepper, chopped
1½ cups finely chopped, cooked chicken
1 piece fresh root ginger, chopped
6 tbsps milk mixed with 2 tsps cornstarch
½ cup sour cream
2 tbsps flaked almonds, toasted

Toppings
Shredded lettuce, grated yellow or Jack cheese
   and Taco Sauce (see recipe)

---

1. Prepare the beef filling as for the Nachos recipe.

2. For the chicken filling, melt 2 tbsps of the butter in a saucepan and add the onion and pepper. Cook until softened.

3. Add the remaining butter to the saucepan and cook the chicken for 5 minutes, turning often. Season and return the onion mixture to the pan, along with the chopped ginger.

4. Add the milk mixture and stir. Bring to the boil and stir until very thick. Mix in the sour cream and almonds and cook gently to heat through, but do not boil.

5. Heat the taco shells on a cookie sheet, open ends downward, in an oven preheated to 350°F, 2-3 minutes.

6. To fill, spoon in about 1 tbsp of beef or chicken filling. Add some shredded lettuce, and some grated cheese, then top with taco sauce.

Shrimp Veracruz

SERVES 4-6

Veracruz is a port on the Gulf of Mexico which lends its name to a variety of colorful seafood dishes.

PREPARATION: 25 mins
COOKING: 15 mins

---

1 tbsp oil
1 onion, chopped
1 large green bell pepper, cut into 1½-inch strips
2-3 green chilies, seeded and chopped
Double quantity Taco Sauce recipe
2 tomatoes, skinned and roughly chopped
12 pimento-stuffed olives, halved
2 tsps capers
¼ tsp ground cumin
Salt
4 cups raw, peeled shrimp
Juice of 1 lime
Boiled rice, to serve

---

1. Heat the oil in a large skillet and add the onion and green bell pepper. Cook until soft but not colored.

Step 2 Add the chilies, taco sauce, tomatoes, olives, capers, cumin, and salt to the pan. Bring to the boil.

2. Add the chilies, taco sauce, tomatoes, olives, capers, cumin, and salt. Bring to the boil. Reduce the heat and simmer 5 minutes.

3. Remove any black veins, from the rounded side of the shrimps with a cocktail stick.

4. Add the shrimp to the sauce and cook until they curl up and turn pink. Add the lime juice to taste and serve with boiled rice.

Enchiladas

SERVES 6

Although fillings and sauces vary, enchiladas (stuffed, rolled tortillas) are one of the tastiest Mexican dishes. Serve with guacamole or refried beans.

PREPARATION: 30 mins
COOKING: 20 mins

---

10 ripe tomatoes, skinned, seeded and chopped
1 small onion, chopped
1-2 chilies, seeded and chopped
1 clove garlic, crushed
1-2 tbsps tomato paste
2 tbsps butter or margarine
2 eggs
1 cup heavy cream
12 ounces ground pork
1 small red bell pepper, chopped
4 tbsps each raisins and pine nuts (piñones)
12 Flour Tortillas (see recipe)
4 tbsps grated Jack or Yellow cheese
Sliced green onions, (scallions) to garnish

1. Place the tomatoes, onion, chilies, garlic and tomato paste in a blender or food processor, and purée until smooth. Melt the butter in a large pan. Add the purée and simmer 5 minutes.

2. Beat together the eggs and cream, mixing well. Add some of the hot purée and mix quickly. Return the mixture to the pan. Heat slowly, stirring constantly, until the mixture thickens. Do not boil.

3. Cook the pork and pepper slowly in a large skillet. Increase the heat when the pork is nearly cooked and fry briskly for a few minutes. Add the raisins, nuts, and seasoning.

4. Combine about one quarter of the sauce with the meat and spoon onto one side of the center of each tortilla. Roll up the tortillas around it, leaving the ends open, and some of the filling showing.

5. Place the enchiladas seam side downward in a baking dish and pour over the remaining sauce, leaving the ends uncovered. Sprinkle with the cheese and bake in an oven preheated to 350°F, 15-20 minutes, or until bubbling. Sprinkle with sliced green onions (scallions) and serve immediately.

Chili con Carne

SERVES 4

Although this dish is a Mexican dish it originated in Texas, before Texas became part of the United States.

PREPARATION: 15 mins
COOKING: 40 mins

---

1 tbsp oil
1 pound ground beef
2 tsps ground cumin
2 tsps mild or hot chili powder
Pinch oregano
Salt, pepper, and a pinch of sugar
¼ tsp garlic powder
2 tbsps all-purpose flour
1 pound canned tomatoes
1 can red kidney beans
Boiled rice, to serve

Step 2 Sprinkle the spice mixture over the browned meat.

Step 3 Add the tomatoes and their liquid to the pan. Use a large spoon or potato masher to break them up.

1. Heat the oil in a large saucepan and brown the meat, breaking it up with a fork as it cooks.

2. Sprinkle with the cumin, chili powder, oregano, salt, pepper, sugar, garlic, and flour. Cook, stirring frequently, over a medium heat for about 3 minutes.

3. Add the tomatoes and their liquid and simmer for 25-30 minutes.

4. Drain the kidney beans and add just before serving, heating through for about 5 minutes. Serve with hot boiled rice.

Flautas

SERVES 6

These long, thin rolled tortillas contain savory fillings and are topped with sour cream.

PREPARATION: 60 mins
COOKING: 30 mins

---

12 Flour Tortillas (see recipe)
1 cup ground or finely chopped chicken
1 tbsp oil
1 small onion, minced
½ green bell pepper, finely chopped
½-1 chili, seeded and finely chopped
½ cup fresh or defrosted frozen sweetcorn
6 black olives, pitted and chopped
½ cup heavy cream
Salt
Taco Sauce, Guacamole (see recipes) and sour
  cream, for toppings

---

1. Wrap the tortillas in aluminum foil and place in a warm oven for 5 minutes to make them pliable.

2. Heat the oil in a medium-sized skillet and add the chicken, onion, and green bell pepper. Cook over a moderate heat, stirring frequently to break up the pieces of chicken.

3. When the chicken is cooked and the

Step 4 Roll up the tortillas and secure with cocktail sticks.

vegetables are softened, add the chili, corn, olives, cream, and salt. Bring to the boil over a high heat and boil rapidly, stirring continuously to reduce and thicken the cream.

4. Place 2 tortillas on a clean work surface, overlapping them by about 2 inches. Spoon some of the chicken mixture onto the tortillas, roll up and secure with wooden cocktail sticks. Repeat the process.

5. Fry the flautas in about ½ inch oil in a large skillet. Do not allow the tortillas to get very brown. Drain on kitchen paper.

6. Arrange the flautas on plates and top with sour cream, guacamole, and taco sauce.

Leg of Lamb with Chili Sauce

SERVES 4

Give roast lamb a Mexican flavor with a tangy orange sauce.

PREPARATION: 15 mins, plus 12-24 hours for the lamb to marinate.
COOKING: 2 hours 20 mins

2¼ pounds leg of lamb

Marinade
1 tsp unsweetened cocoa
½ tsp cayenne pepper
½ tsp ground cumin
½ tsp paprika
½ tsp ground oregano
⅔ cup water
⅔ cup orange juice
⅔ cup dry red wine
1 clove of garlic, crushed
2 tbsps brown sugar

1 tbsp cornstarch mixed with 2 tbsps water
Orange slices and coriander (cilantro) to garnish

1. Mix together the marinade ingredients, and pour them over the lamb, turning it to coat. Cover and refrigerate for 12-24 hours, turning occasionally.

2. Drain the lamb, reserving the marinade, and place in a roasting pan. Cook, basting occasionally with the marinade, in an oven preheated to 350°F, for about 2 hours or until cooked to taste.

3. Remove the lamb to a serving platter and keep warm. Skim off the fat from the roasting pan. Pour remaining marinade into the pan and bring to the boil, stirring.

4. Add some of the hot liquid to the cornstarch mixture then gradually stir into the pan and bring back to the boil. Cook, stirring constantly, until thickened and clear. Add some water if necessary.

5. Garnish the lamb with orange slices and sprigs of coriander (cilantro). Pour over some of the sauce and serve the rest separately.

Tostadas

MAKES 12

These are popular all over Mexico and the toppings reflect the food available in each area. They are delicious, but difficult to eat!

PREPARATION: 40 mins
COOKING: 15 mins

2 tsps oil
1 pound ground beef or pork
2 tsps chili powder
1 tsp ground cumin
1 tsp ground coriander (cilantro)
1 can refried beans
1 package tostada shells

Toppings
Shredded lettuce
Grated Yellow or Jack cheese
Tomatoes, seeded and chopped
Sour cream
Olives
Cooked, peeled shrimp
Green onions (scallions), chopped
Taco Sauce (see recipe)

1. Heat the oil in a medium sized skillet. Add the ground beef or pork and fry quickly to brown, then cook over a moderate heat 8-10 minutes. Sprinkle on the spices and cook 1-2 minutes.

2. Reheat the beans and place the tostada shells on a cookie sheet. Heat for 2-3 minutes in a moderate oven.

3. Spread 1-2 tbsps of the beans on each tostada shell.

4. Top each shell with some of the beef mixture.

5. Add the topping ingredients in different combinations and serve immediately.

Step 4 Spoon some beef mixture over the beans, pushing it down gently.

Minute Steaks with Taco Sauce

SERVES 6

Prepare the sauce in advance and keep it on hand to add last-minute spice to a meal.

PREPARATION: 15 mins
COOKING: 30 mins

Full quantity Taco Sauce recipe
2 tbsps butter or margarine
2 tbsps oil
6 frying steaks
Salt and pepper
1 cup button mushrooms, left whole
Minced parsley or coriander (cilantro) leaves

1. Prepare the taco sauce according to the recipe. Heat the butter and oil together in a large skillet.

Step 2 Sauté the steaks for 2-3 minutes on each side, or until cooked to taste.

Step 3 Add the whole mushrooms to the pan, and sauté until lightly browned.

2. Season the steaks with salt and pepper and fry two or three at a time for 2-3 minutes on each side, or to taste.

3. Remove the steaks to a warm serving dish and add the mushrooms to the pan. Sauté over a high heat to brown lightly, remove and keep warm.

4. Drain most of the fat from the pan and add in the taco sauce. Place over a low heat until just bubbling. Spoon it over the steaks.

5. Top the steaks with the sautéed mushrooms and sprinkle with parsley or coriander (cilantro) before serving.

Mexican Chocolate Flan

SERVES 4

Flan in Mexico is a molded custard with a caramel sauce. Chocolate and cinnamon is a favorite flavor combination.

PREPARATION: 30 mins
COOKING: 40 mins, plus overnight chilling

½ cup superfine sugar
2 tbsps water
Juice of ½ lime
2 squares semi-sweet chocolate
1¼ cups milk
1 cinnamon stick
2 whole eggs
2 egg yolks
4 tbsps granulated sugar

---

1. Combine the first superfine sugar with the water and lime juice in a small, heavy-based saucepan.

2. Cook over a gentle heat, stirring until the sugar dissolves. Then without stirring, bring the syrup to the boil and cook until golden-brown and caramelized.

3. While preparing the syrup, heat 4 ramekins or individual soufflé dishes in an oven preheated to 350°F. When the syrup is ready, pour into the hot ramekins, and swirl to coat

the sides and base evenly. Leave to cool at room temperature.

4. Chop the chocolate into small pieces and heat with the milk and cinnamon, stirring occasionally to help the chocolate dissolve.

5. Whisk the whole eggs and the yolks together with the remaining sugar until slightly frothy. Gradually whisk in the hot chocolate milk. Remove the cinnamon stick.

6. Strain the chocolate custard carefully into the ramekins and stand them in a roasting pan filled with enough hand-hot water to come halfway up the sides of the dishes.

7. Carefully place the roasting pan in the oven, and bake the custards for 20-25 minutes, or until they have just set, and a knife inserted in the center of the custard comes out clean.

8. Cool at room temperature and refrigerate for several hours or overnight before serving. Loosen the custards by running a knife around the edges and invert onto individual serving plates. If necessary, shake the custard to allow it to drop out.

Tropical Fruit Salad

SERVES 6

A refreshing mixture of exotic fruits is the most popular dessert in Mexico. Add tequila or Triple Sec to the syrup for a special occasion.

PREPARATION: 45 mins

½ cantaloupe or honeydew melon, cubed or made into balls
½ small fresh pineapple, peeled, cored, and cubed or sliced
½ cup fresh strawberries, hulled and halved (leave whole, if small)
1 mango, peeled, and sliced or cubed
1 cup watermelon, seeded and cubed
½ cup guava or papaya, peeled and cubed
2 oranges, peeled and segmented
1 prickly pear (cactus fruit), peeled and sliced (optional)
½ cup superfine sugar
½ cup water
Grated rind and juice of 1 lime
2 tbsps chopped pecans, to decorate

1. To make melon balls, cut the melons in half. Scoop out seeds and discard them. To use a melon baller, press the cutting edge firmly into the melon flesh and twist around to scoop out round pieces.

2. It is easier to core the pineapple if it is first

Step 2 Cut the pineapple into quarters and remove the core with a serrated knife.

cut into quarters. Use a serrated fruit knife to cut the point off the quarter, removing the core. Slice off the peel and remove any brown "eyes" with the tip of a potato peeler. Cut into slices or cubes and mix with the other fruit.

3. Dissolve the sugar in the water over a gentle heat and when the mixture is no longer grainy, bring to the boil and cook 1 minute, then leave to cool completely.

4. Add the lime rind and juice to the sugar syrup and pour this over the prepared fruit. Refrigerate well before serving, then sprinkle with the chopped nuts.

Mango Whip

SERVES 6

To cool the palate after a spicy Mexican meal, the taste of mango, lime, ginger, and cream is a perfect combination.

PREPARATION: 20 mins, plus 1 hour
chilling

---

2 ripe mangoes
1 small piece fresh root ginger, peeled and
  shredded
½ cup confectioner's sugar, sifted
Juice of ½ lime
⅔ cup heavy cream

Step 3 Whip the cream until soft peaks form.

1. Cut the mangoes in half, cutting either side of the large central stone. Reserve two slices,

Step 1 Cut the mangoes in half, slicing around the large central stone, and scoop out the flesh.

then scoop out the flesh into a bowl, blender, or food processor.

2. Add the ginger, confectioner's sugar, and lime juice and purée in the blender or food processor until smooth.

3. Whip the cream until soft peaks form and then fold into the mango purée.

4. Divide the mixture between 6 sundae glasses and refrigerate for 1 hour before serving.

5. Cut the reserved mango slices into 6 smaller slices or pieces and use to decorate the dessert.

Index